Written with Colors
Drawn with Words

Written with Colors
Drawn with Words

Al Nashashibi

AlNashashibi, INC.

Written with Colors
Drawn with Words

ISBN 978-0-9891122-0-8

For information contact
AlNashashibi, Inc.
www.alnashashibi.com
3166 Midway Drive, suite #102
San Diego, California 92110
Artwork, illustrations and design by
AlNashashibi

INTRODUCTION

If you visit Fairouz Café and Gallery on Midway Drive in San Diego, a family owned restaurant with a superb Eastern Mediterranean buffet, you can enjoy your meal while surrounded by the distinctive artwork of Ibrahim AlNashashibi, who opened the restaurant in 1984 and has exhibited his paintings in at least ten countries. And you may be welcomed by the artist, a warm-hearted, shaggy-haired bear of a man, or another member of his family, who are frequently on the scene.

Recurrent themes in the paintings are peace, relationships between people, a sense of the past, and a love of the old city of Jerusalem, where Ibrahim was born and raised and where his family has deep roots. His father's ancestors were hereditary supervisors of the Muslim holy places in Jerusalem, his maternal grandfather's family supervised King David's tomb, and his mother's mother was a Sephardic Jew whose ancestors settled in Jerusalem after the expulsion from Spain in 1492; she never learned much Arabic but spoke Judeo-Spanish (aka Latino and Judezmo) and English to Ibrahim, whose painting style reflects her quilt patterns.

Although he knew even in childhood that he could paint, painting was discouraged, and Ibrahim opted for a career in law. With a law degree from Beirut Arab University, he held a responsible position for many years at a major insurance company in Kuwait. His conscience, however, kept him awake each night as he judged himself for the unfair and deceptive acts of the day, especially in his dealings with clients. Caught between the pursuit of power and comfort and the needs of his soul, Ibrahim sought other options.

One option was to sign a five-year contract in 1981 as a legal consultant to an insurance company in Dubai, where he dealt with company officials, not clients. Even before that, while he was still working in Kuwait, he decided to immigrate to the United States and commute to the Middle East to the extent that his green card allowed. So in 1978 he brought his wife and infant son to St. Petersburg, Florida, where his wife's brother lived, and built a house and bought rental properties there. In 1983 (commuting now to Dubai, not Kuwait), he became a U.S. citizen.

Then, on a visit to his wife's sister in San Diego, he fell in love with the city even before the plane landed. Although Jerusalem will always be Ibrahim's first home, he feels that San Diego is his second home. His new plan was to open the restaurant, take a year to save money and study English, and then complete a doctorate in international law at an American university so that he could teach and, in that way, find peace with himself.

New discoveries came thick and fast. First, he had to be on hand in the restaurant. Next, he found he was connecting with his customers as people, not as clients. Here were the relationships he had been seeking in his professional life, and they helped him to decide to quit the practice of law once his contract in Dubai was complete. Although an end to living and working on two continents must have brought him a measure of peace, it put an intolerable strain on his marriage, which ended in a painful divorce.

It was during that time that he started painting, turning the restaurant into a studio in the slack hours between lunch and dinner. Having never taken a formal art course, he became his viewers' student and learned to paint from their feedback. He says their compliments encouraged his inner child to come out and play on canvas.

There was one more discovery for Ibrahim in that momentous decade of the 1980s, as he began to bring his parents, brothers, and sister-in-law to live with him in San Diego (and help at the restaurant). One day one of his customers brought along his sister, Hafida Krim, who had just come from her home in Morocco to stay with him while she recovered from the sudden death of their father. Three years later, Ibrahim and Hafida were married, and this book is dedicated to her.

Hafida grew up in Rabat, the capital of Morocco; her father was Algerian and her mother came from a well-known Moroccan family. At sixteen Hafida went to England to work and study English; then she attended college in Paris. Well-read and well-informed, she loved to travel and worked for Royal Morocco Airlines, where she served on the king's private plane. We remember her as a quiet, refined lady who kept mostly to herself and worked for many hours on Ibrahim's paintings. In 1997, when he returned from two months in Jerusalem, she surprised him with twenty-nine of her own paintings, and sold most of them.

Hafida passed away in the spring of 2009, having chosen to return to Morocco after her cancer was declared terminal; she is buried in the family plot in Casablanca. Staying by her side during the months of her final coma, Ibrahim feels he received a parting gift from his beloved when he became inspired to write. He immediately planned out a novel and started writing; five years later, it is still in progress. At the same time, in his grief he began writing letters to his departed love, and after a while he shared some of them with his brother Rami, who told him his letters were poems.

So Ibrahim began intentionally to write poems to Hafida, and before long other kinds of poems emerged, as he found that some creative ideas call for expression in paintings and others, in poetry. From memory and imagination, he wrote about love between a man and a woman, both praise and critiques of love. More philosophical poems explore the life of the artist and the world he inhabits. The present selection brings together poems and drawings on each of these themes.

John Hitchcock
San Diego, 2014

Table Of Contents

1 Hafida

2 Affirming Love

3 Questioning Love

4 Life

5 The World

Acknowledgment

The writings of this book owe their inspiration to my grief that was born from the death of my beloved wife, friend, and muse Hafida Krim AlNashashibi.

My heartfelt gratitude goes to my friends and editors, John Hitchcock and David Feldman, and their wives Ellie and Betty, for the encouragement they gave me.

I also owe a huge debt to my late father, Shafiq AlNashashibi, and my loving mother Samira AlDajani, who believed in my work since my youth.

My heart sends love and appreciation to my dearest brothers, Sami and Rami, and to my dear cousin Sahar, and sisters, Amal and Fawzyah, who allowed me the time and support I needed to create my paintings and writings.

Also thanks to the younger generation in the family, my children Rakan, Tamara and Fares. Along with my nieces and nephews for making me love to challenge their talents.

And to all my friends in San Diego and abroad who supported and embraced me and my family with their love and encouragement for the last thirty years.

Written with Colors
Drawn with Words

I came to life with a lot of thoughts and feelings
some to be written with colors
And
some to be drawn with words

AlNashashibi

My Story

When I was not able to talk, I screamed with colors
I was five years old when I started talking
almost as a beginner
My mother was worried
that I would never be able to speak
I never knew whether I had a speech problem
or I was busy discovering the world
To me, the children of my age were childish
and the elders were living in the clouds of ignorance

So, I chose to live in my own world of imagination
Later I faced life's realities
Everyone I encounter wants to rebuild me
in his or her image
Which is different from how I see myself
So I was rebellious
And my mind spoke the truth, my truth
Which was rejected by their beliefs
And that didn't help
So I swam with the current of their thoughts
And disabled my dreams

For years I wore masks that didn't fit my soul
And succeeded by the power of my positions
in the world
But my soul didn't rest
Until I started using art as my alphabet
of communication
And I became a free human
Wearing no masks
And full of happiness of visions
And the joy of creativity

In this book of poetry
I speak to you directly from my heart and mind
To your heart and mind
Hoping to get connected
With love and peace

AlNashashibi

1 Hafida

The Moroccan Lady

Oh, beloved Hafida,
in the years we were one
you were
the wife
the lover
and the friend.
You taught me how to enjoy gourmet food,
which you prepared for us,
and you were the one who made my life easy
and made me love my existence.
The roses you cared for
and the music you planted in our nest
encouraged my creativity to nurture
seeds of peace.
In every move I made
you were my doctor, psychologist and advisor
and the teacher who laid the light on my path.
You were the shoulder that carried my fear,
my insecurities and my mistakes.
Strong like iron and soft like a feather, you were.
You were not just a woman
but an angel from Morocco.
You were everything in my life
and I salute you
Proud spirit of Morocco.

For You I Will Sing

I am a poet
Not a singer
But for your memory I will sing
My song will be a portrait of your beauty
Written with words
In the colors of my love
For you

In My Dark Moments

I ask
Why love was created
With the brush of a rainbow
And wiped by the storm of death

Beyond The Clouds Of Death

I had no time
Or opportunity
To ask you before
Your departure
What is beyond the clouds of death?

You let me sink
In the black ocean of grief
For years
But last night
In your visit to my dream
I understood

On earth you were tired
And now in the horizon of the angels
You are a spirit
Swimming in the fountain of youth
Free of the chains of pain

In The Deep Ocean Of Sadness

In the deep ocean of sadness
In the molten volcano of anger
In the remote desert with no compass
In the tornado of confusion
In the wilderness of regret
In the falls of grieving eyes
At the summit of deterioration
I dwell
Ever since you left

After Five Years Of Your Passing

At that moment of pain
I lost the feeling of time
And my attachments to life
Like a tree that died
Except for one promising leaf
Like a spring fully dry
But for a few drops of water
Like a dying heart
That refuses to fade
I keep your memory
Safe in my heart
Until we meet
Again

Hafida 2008   AL Nashashibi 2014

When the Sky Cried

Things happen for a reason
And this one was the greatest.
The sorrowful pain of your passing caused
The cry of the sky,
The eclipse of the sun,
And of the moon,
The death of happiness
The sadness of the birds
The grief of the butterflies
The tears of the ocean
And the bleeding of nature
All wept for your loss.
No life, not even a breath
Except...
The smile drawn on your lips
Just like a red rose blooming in the desert
Of sadness
The lips that I gave a last kiss
When my hands laid you
In your eternal bedroom
Where my heart cried goodbye

I Love The Past Of My Past

When I search the past of my past
I see you standing
In the future
Of my life
I see you as the bird
That flies around me
Like a golden crown
To protect
My dreams
I sec you as an angel
That embraces
My safety
I love the past of my past
For you are the past
I wish to keep
In my future

Distant Dreams

As a boy in my small bedroom
I looked at the high ceiling
And wondered
Where dreams come from
And how they arrive at my pillow
For in my mind dreams were
Aliens come from afar
For chosen kids
To tell them magical narratives
For them to sleep softly
Now my dreams have become
Visitors I seek to catch
And wish to receive
For I need your presence in my dreams
To feel safe
And face my next day
Without you

Dancing Alone

It was a very special dream;
in fact it was two dreams in one,
exactly as if I were conscious and truly living it.

In the first dream
I found myself preparing the room for us to dance;
I pushed the furniture back to the walls
and played our favorite Sinatra song.

I embraced you gently,
put your left palm in mine
and my right hand on your delicate waist.

My cheek was enjoying the warmth of your face
and my heart was pounding happily into yours.

When the music came to end,
I woke to find myself living my second dream.
I was wearing my pajamas,
holding your wedding dress in my hands
and dancing alone.

When I Prepare My Morning Coffee

I look at my empty cup
Impatiently asking for coffee to feed its hunger
I ask myself
What step should I take?
My experience with morning coffees is limited
Because
When you were around
It was always given to me
Wrapped in love
And enriched with a
Slice of a French cake
Or a delicious Moroccan cookie
My life then was complete
And I was in Heaven
But now after you
Nothing makes sense
And my
Morning coffee
Has no taste

Mirage

In San Diego my love for you was born,
in Morocco it grew up,
and when you passed,
my love for you matured.

Oh Darling,
your visits to my dreams feed my heart with
more love and my mind with peace.

Oh Darling,
in my last dream we walked in the narrow
alleys of the old city of Casablanca.
My eyes were full of your beauty,
colored with the tones of the history of art,
the art of love and peace.

There, Darling,
my senses were enjoying the embrace of your soul
and the unity of our spirits.
God blessed our journey,
the journey that ended
when my eyes opened
and my dream was a mirage.

For You I Shall Return

When I come back to life,
I will choose to be a bird.
A bird with long, strong wings.
Wings to fly you to the high skies of freedom
And carry you to the mountains of imagination
And to the oceans of your heart's desire.
And at night when you go to sleep,
I will be there on the window sill,
Protecting you from the unpleasant dreams.

Do You Still Love Me

Do you still love me?
Aren't you angry that I died?
And left you alone in the ocean of loneliness
When you needed my love
That is what she asked him
In the dream where they were one
Yes I did
When I was swimming alone
In the river of my selfishness
But when my heart recognized
Your suffering
I let you go
To the land of rest
That is what he answered
In the dream when they were one

Thursday

Thursday was my best day of the week
The morning sun was always soft
Just like your rosy cheeks under the big hat
Walking in the forest
Around the lake of our love
As we named it
Hand in hand
Except when we stand still
To enjoy a long sweet kiss
When walkers happily stop
To give us words of
Compliment
We thankfully smile as an answer
But now I walk alone
Reliving those beautiful moments

Before You

Before you I was a man
Carrying a load of mountains
And looking at life through thick gray lenses
Nothing cast a shadow
And nothing was green
My tears of sorrow were falling unbidden
And the fear of life was controlling my emotions
That was me before you
Then I met you and
The birds of my heart woke up to sing the melody of love
And I became larger than my depressed being
I learned to cry for joy
And you made me the master of happiness
You and only you
Grabbed my negativity
And with the power of a magician
Turned it into the wonders of
Love

Longing For You

Years after your
Passing
The manly hunger in me
Sought a female companion
So I searched the earth
And found
You are
The only lady
Of my heart

Symphony Of Love

There are three of us, me,
You and her
She is here
Sitting on the remaining string of my heart
Conducting music that carries
Her talent and my signature
For you to read
A reading of the true emotions of two lovers
One on Earth and the other in Heaven,
Composing the eternal symphony of love

Like A Tattoo

Like a tattoo attached to my mind
My love for you is engraved
In the four rooms of my heart
Like a living shadow,
I keep walking behind
He goes fast
I go fast
He slows down
I do the same
And when we both get tired
We hug each other
In the memory of you
While you are in Heaven
Looking down at us and happily
Saying
Blessed be your unity

You Never Left

In the house
I live with your memory
Happy and content

Your existence is so powerful
In the oxygen I breathe your scent
Fresh as if you still live here
In the closet your dresses are
Sleeping gently

In your picture wearing the bikini
I can see your healthy breast
Before it was eaten by cancer

The cat wakes up to look into my eyes
Eats her food and goes to the corner
To sleep and dream of you again

The plants around the house
Turn toward me and smile
The counter top in the kitchen
Is shining the way you prefer

And I
Thank my blessings
For you never
Left my heart

Hafida

You are away
But not far away
My mind is an honest
Album for your living face
And my heart is an excellent
Ode for your never-forgotten emotions
My love for you
Is growing
By looking through the pages
Of my mind
And listening to the rhythms
Of my heart

See You Forever

Don't say goodbye, it is not our destiny.
Say, "See you," It feeds my heart with hope
and rewards my soul with peace.
In your path I will plant roses of love
to blossom your days with joy;
Blessed be your journey.
Don't say goodbye, rather say,
"See you forever."

2 Affirming Love

When I Become A Poet

When I become a poet
And gain control of the language
I will write a poem for you
When I learn the alphabet of notes
And walk through the rhythms
I will compose a song for you
But now
I am still immature
And all I can say is simply
I love you

If I Were A Bird

If I were a bird
I wouldn't leave your window.
I would sing so that you sleep like an angel
and wake you up with a great energy.
If I were a bird
I would warble to you songs of the peace from paradise
and whisper into your heart that I love you.
I would spread my wings like a pillow
to be soft for your supple neck
so you have a gentler sleep
for your spirit to enjoy heavenly dreams.
If I were a bird, this is what I would do,
But I was born a man,
a man who wishes to be that bird.

I Wanted

I wanted to place the whole world in your palms
But my arms were too short
So please accept this red rose instead.

My desire was to bring you the golden stars
But the sky was much higher than my reach.

The rainbow was my target to color your life
But it disappeared before I was able to catch it.

I asked the birds to sing for you
But gathering them would take their freedom away.

So, please accept my endless love.

It Is A Beautiful Day

It is a beautiful day
It is my birthday
The sun is embracing my heart with warmth
and the sky is showering my spirit with kindness
The birds are singing songs of joy
while jumping from branch to branch
The butterflies are happily traveling
between the flowers
to plant love and peace throughout the garden
It is a beautiful day
It is my birthday
My happiness is complete
and needs nothing
Except
Your presence

Trust Me

Trust all my deeds
The ones you understand
And the ones you don't
Trust my decisions
The ones you agree with
And the ones you don't
For I trust everything we do
To build the future of our love
Brick by brick
And dream with a dream
To secure our minds
From the attack
Of the storm of doubts
That may invade
The golden nest
That we erected
Around our
United hearts

Our Secrets

I am in love with our secrets
The big ones and the little
I am in love with our sins
The ones we may be forgiven for
And the ones that we won't
For all were written in the book of our destiny
From which we harvested our joy

The First Love

It has been said
No love survives
Except the first
I would say
Every love is always the
First
But my love for you is
The last

When My Fingers Plant The Seeds

When my fingers
Touch your skin
A high voltage
Of emotions
Strikes my
Heart
So I become
Like a horse
Strong and
Anxious

When my eyes
Explore your body
My mind dances
On the rhythms
Of the landscape of
The hills and valleys
Of your beauty

So
My fingers plant
The seeds
And my eyes
Harvest
The blooms

The Land Of Purple Dreams

To the land of purple dreams take my heart
Where the birds fly free
And imagination has no borders
Where the clouds are soft as silk
And love is forever innocent
Take me along with you on the wings of hope
For a journey with no return
So together we will live in the land of purple dreams
Where the colors of hate do not exist

Happy Birthday To You

I went to the forest and asked the birds
   to join me
   to sing Happy Birthday to you

I went to the gardens and asked the flowers
   to create from their beauty
   a bouquet of love for you

I went to the ocean and asked the waves
   to dance to the symphony
   played by the wind just for you

I went to the skies and collected the stars
   to build a magical crown for you

I went to the bottom of my heart
   to celebrate your grace
   embedded in its veins

I went to the mountain of wishes
   and asked God
   to bless you

The Piano

While you were playing the piano,
I heard heavenly music composed by an angel from the sky
of creativity.
Your fingers were not but emotions, pouring life into the
keyboard.
My eyes were dancing to the rhythms of your genius,
and my heart was breathing joy.
My lips slowly sipped my drink,
And just as I reached the bottom of the glass,
Your fingers left the keys
and I fell in love with you.

3 Questioning Love

Love is like medicine
We must study the side effects
First

AlNashashibi

Mirrors

We are mirrors of our personalities
I look at your heart and see
My picture
And you look at my heart and see
Yours
If we see nice pictures
Then we are in love
If we don't
We should break
Our mirrors
Peacefully

Multiple Destinies

It was a joyful destiny
When we met
And when we fell in love
But life has different directions
For everyone
And not
One size fits all
We don't see things through the same
Mind lenses
None of us is absolutely right or
Absolutely wrong
Sometimes the view we see
Is drawn by an illusion
Has the look of
Love
And has the taste of
Love
Which we blindly follow
Until we are touched by awareness
And find
It was our destiny to meet
And it is our destiny to separate

The Bird Is Flying Away

The bird you raised in my heart
Is flying out and away
From the tiny cage you built for his wings
The borders you tried to keep his freedom within
Were unnatural to his nature
And you were unable to get him
Domesticated
So his journey started
To discover a
Better nest

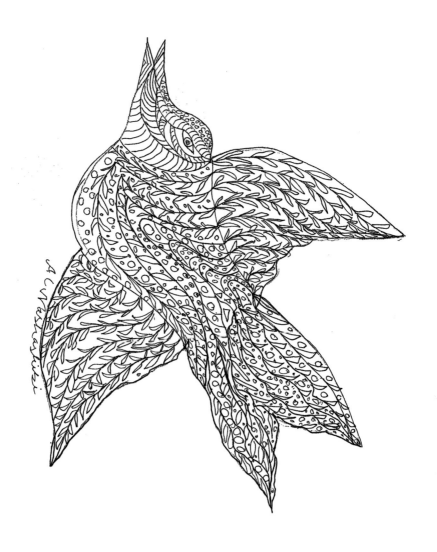

Two people were looking at a man who was crying and laughing at the same time
The first one said, "I am sure he is crying for the loss of his love"
The other one said, "I think he is laughing for joy over that loss"

AlNashashibi

I Wonder

Sometimes I wonder
If you really love me
Or you love to be
Loved

Sometimes you make me
Think
If love is all about giving
Or only about receiving
And if it is the feeling of the heart
Or the product of the ego

Because
On our last date
You said
I love you because you love me
And for being gentle
With me
I love you because you understand
My wants and needs
And embrace my changeable moods

So you made me debate
If you love me
Or you are
In love with your ego

He Told Me

He told me she loves him
And he was her choice of love
He told me he loves me
And I was his choice of love
The length of lies is short
So the truth was revealed
And we both discovered
He loves but himself

A Different Language

He claimed
Our bad relationship
Is coming from
Our poor communication
She thought and countered
I believe
We communicate well
But the problem is that
We use a language
That our brains
Can't comprehend
And our emotions can't deal with
So when our love
Tries hard to gather us
Into its nest
Our feelings
Put us in the Hell
Of anger
Where our egos
Become the masters of
The stage
And we become
The soldiers
Of War

I Love You, She Said

She said
I love you
He answered
I love you more
She questioned
Are you sure?
Definitely
He answered
Why?
She asked
Because your love for me
Is measured by how good I am
For your needs
When my love for you is
Unconditional

Late Arrival

Your flight of love
Is landing late
All terminals of
My heart are closed
You deserve the best welcome
But my emotions went to rest
And the runway of my desires
Is under construction
So please find a new
Landing strip

The Angels

You told me
You are like the angels of Heaven
Never to cheat
On me

So I liked to believe
Your promise
And felt secure

But when I asked the angels
They told me
Some lovers can't be
Trusted

Regain My Peace

Every night,
I asked God to tell me what was best for me to do.
That was my practice until I met you.
Then, I asked not God but my heart,
for my fear
was that God might forbid me to love you.
Instead,
I followed my emotions
and took the magical journey you promised.
Later,
to regain my lost peace,
I went back to seek God.

Our Love Is Boring

Let's go back to the beginning, when our eyes first met
When we only saw the beauty in each other
When for you
I was a genius and my mind was brilliant
And for me
You were the queen of earth, the muse of my imagination
When my thoughts were invitations
And my spirit was created by Angels
Let's go back to when we accepted who we were
And not who we wanted each other to be
Remember the old tall tree in the backyard of our first
home
Where we had our naps while the birds
Were singing the song of love for us
Remember the ocean breeze gently hitting our faces
And how joyfully we used to laugh
Come closer and let's enjoy life again

Love Is Good

Love is good
Ownership is bad
Love is freedom
Ownership is a prison
To occupy the heart, mind and talent
That we were born with

Love comes with birth
Pure like our spirits
Born from the womb of nature
To live free

Ownership was created
By cultural systems
For control

And was called
Marriage

4 Life

It is our choice to create for ourselves
The Castle of happiness
Or the Cocoon of misery

AlNashashibi

The Train

I love you and always will
You were the treasure added to my life
And the last chapter of my existence

But your path is going north
When my path is going south

All directions are good

But the train of our life is in need
Of parallel tracks

Love Is To Be Learned

She thinks
love is natural
we are born with it
but without nourishment it might
Vanish

He thinks
we come to life with an empty mind
like a brand new book
and life writes on it our experiences
the good and the bad

Some think
we are the product of many lives
some with a great love experience
and some with a rotten one

I think
all thoughts are valuable
and I am still
Learning

A Decision To Retire

One calm, relaxed and contented morning
I reached the top of my pyramid of success.
And with full awareness, I decided to retire.
But the question was more clever than my thoughts.
How can the artist retire from Art?
And a poet divorce Poetry?
How can I be another person?
Who will portray your gorgeous eyes?
Who will celebrate the birth of a new life each day
And join nature to praise the glory of joy?

"The talent you have been given
is not your personal property,"
An inner voice told me.
"Rather it is to share with mankind
The colors you melt in your images
to uplift the hearts of your beholders
And the melody you compose in your poems
to whisper into the souls of readers,
These were the reasons why you were given talent
With the condition that you never stop.
For this is your destiny,
To live after you die."

The Muse

The Muse sinks through the
Window of my mind
She dictates
And
I write
A poem

Life is a remote virgin island designed
differently for each of us
And waiting to be explored

AlNashashibi

The Clouds

The clouds of my mind
Are always pregnant with a woman
And at the right season she falls into my
Arms
Sometimes the wind brings her from the east
And at other times she comes from the west
Sometimes from the north
And at other times from the south
They all are perfect for my needs
I wrap them carefully with tender love
And they become my muses
Some are gentle
So my poems are nice
Some are tough
So my poems are hard
Some are materialistic
So I don't create
Even a song
But all of them
When they discover the poet in me
Leave me
To live
My own dreams
Alone

In My Last Dream

In my last dream I heard a voice
There were some pictures
But all were dark
The voice was so powerful
Pure as the truth
Clear as freedom
And loud as a scream
The voice declared
"Life is an endless chain of chores"
In the morning, when I woke
I smiled and said my daily prayer
"Yesterday I was happy, today I am happier"
And went on to create one more great day

The Love Of God

I am positive of my beliefs
Confident with no doubts
That God loves me
I was born in Jerusalem, the best city of the world
And live in San Diego, the second-best city of the world
My heart is filled with love, so no fear can enter
Content and relaxed now
For I went through all pains needed
To reach the top of the pyramid of awareness
So I can be an artist
And thank God for His gifts

In The Garden

In the garden I walk my morning
Free as though newly born
With a clear mind
And blossomed spirit
I enjoy my existence
The tender new leaves
Welcome my wet fingers
While the young butterfly
Pushes back at my intrusion
Seeking her rightful place
On the flowers
Gently and with respect
I let them embrace
And my hand goes to pick an orange
So my eyes meet the singing bird
Looking at me while continuing his
Symphony of love
Happily I listen
And live the magic
Of the
Garden

The Cat

As if I had no choice
I found myself living with my son's cat
It wasn't my decision
But I inherited her
Before
I was the king of my property
Now she is the ruler
And according to her mood I act
When I want to paint
She jumps all over my paints
When I try to play a song
Her meow overpowers the voice
And if I dare to watch a movie
She starts scratching my couch
So for me to live in peace
I moved out

The Beauty Of Dignity

The beauty of dignity
Just like the truth
Has multiple faces
But one shines overall
And its finest face shines on
The best friend of man
The Arabian Horse
He has a sculpted body
To gracefully race the wind
Across the fields of freedom
With a neck that reaches above the skies of gentle pride
He has an honest soul
Embedded in his unseen wings of purity
That allows him to fly above all other creatures
No one can fool him
Not because of his intelligence
But for his sharp sense of the truth
Which makes him a friend
And not a slave

Now at my age
I laugh
At my youth
When I thought
I knew everything

AlNashashibi

We Write Our Stories

We all write our stories in
Life
Consciously or unconsciously
For life doesn't deal with us
Individually
In richness we proudly say
We Did it !
In poverty we sadly cry
Life Did It !!
In the pyramid of success
We Did It !!!
In the depth of failure
Life Did It !!!!
On the ocean of joy
We Did It !!!!!
In the lake of depression
Life Did It !!!!!!
So
Our Life
Who is running it?

Suffering

One of those rare days
My son and his family
Came to share with me
The joyous holiday
Everyone was happy
Except my grandson
I took him aside
And asked
What is bothering you?
As if he had been expecting the question
His quick answer was
I am suffering from life
I asked
How old are you?
He said
I am fourteen
I said
I am eighty-nine

Book Learned

I am so sorry that you wasted your genius
By traveling through the alleys of books
Books that were taken from other books
Coated with a new manipulation
That misleads those who don't know
There is no genius
Without a genius work
A work to be created completely
From the depth of your own consciousness
And not from the intelligence of others

Dementia

Dementia is not our enemy
Rather it comes when we get weary
Of what life brings to us
It's our gift from God
For the relief we need
From
This troubled
World

Do You Know What You Want?

You want peace
But peace is like a swing
Sometimes real
But mostly an illusion
You want love
Sometimes real
But mostly an illusion
So maybe you are
Sometimes real
But mostly an illusion

You Think You Know Me

I am not what you think I am
Because
I don't know who is living in
My body
So how could you?

Sometimes I am the son
Of today
And other times I came
Gradually from the past
Of the past

Sometimes I feel
I was a seed in the womb
Of the wind
And other times
I was born from the tears
Of the ocean

Sometimes I was created by
The smile of a child
Like the cooing of a dove
And other times I am an explosion
Like the scream of a victim

So quit thinking
That you know me
And join me in
Searching

Who am l ?

Waiting

A tribute to Robin Williams

We live life waiting for good things
To happen
And we call them
Hopes

We live life waiting for bad things
To disappear
And we call them
Wishes

We live life waiting
For hopes and wishes
To happen

But

While we are waiting
Nothing happens
And
Death comes faster

Is Life An Illusion?

Sadness, anger and hate
Are real
So they live in us forever
But

Joy, happiness and relaxation
Pass through our moments
So fast and so untraceable
Like the sweet breeze of a fleeting deception
Is it because
They are an illusion?

Our subconscious perfectly relives
The most painful of memories
As if they injure us again

But our minds
Hardly remember the thin layers
Of happiness
And

Why do we live believing
We were victims
Of everyone and everything
But not victims
Of our own mistakes?

So
The painful side of life is
Real
And the joyful side is
An illusion

5 The World

Politicians are best at creating a problem
for every solution.

AlNashashibi

Back To Nature

At the end of a tiring day
I entered the kingdom of sleep
A painful scene was introduced to my mind
it started with love and ended with hate
hope was stolen and freedom was taken away
help became so expensive none could attain it
narrow paths and blocked ways
walls higher than the sky
and borders that grew into a maze
good turned to bad and right became wrong
friends were considered enemies
and enemies united against the good
spirituality disappeared and materialism was revealed
my loud crying woke me to find myself
grabbing a piece of cheese,
some water, and a loaf of bread
and I went to the forest
leaving civilized people behind

I Listened

I listened to the teachers who educate our children
  And found they need to learn what they teach

I listened to the politicians talking about the law
    that governs us
  And found them living out of it

I listened to the religious leaders
  And found them creating commandments
    God didn't give

I listened to the philosophers
  And found them talking to the people
    who live in the clouds

I listened to peace activists
  And found them searching for their own
    inner self-peace

I listened to the scientists
  And found them scientifically needing improvement

I listened to the artists
  And found them seeking freedom
    that does not exist but in their imagination

I listened to the doctors
  And found them busy listening to the orders
    of the pharmaceutical tycoons

I listened to the psychologists
  And found that we the people should vote for a law

that requires a clinical test
  For them prior to practicing

I listened to the social media
  And found that the road they are leading humanity to
    is the laboratory of robots

  After all the listening
I listened to my mind and grew from being a lawyer to an
  Artist
I listened to my heart and decided to continue being happy

The Gate Of History

In a peaceful summer dawn, mother Jerusalem gave me birth
And with spirituality she fed my soul
In this greatest city I was lucky to grow and learn
And the best lesson I learned from Aunt Surayah
An aunt that God intended for me to meet in my newest life
For a reason to discover myself and why I was born
That was in a peaceful summer sunset
When Aunt Surayah asked me why I was lonely
"I am afraid to die" was my answer
Oh that was easy, she then said
I will tell you the secret to make you live forever
"Do good deeds to humanity, people will love you, put you
in History
Where you will never die."

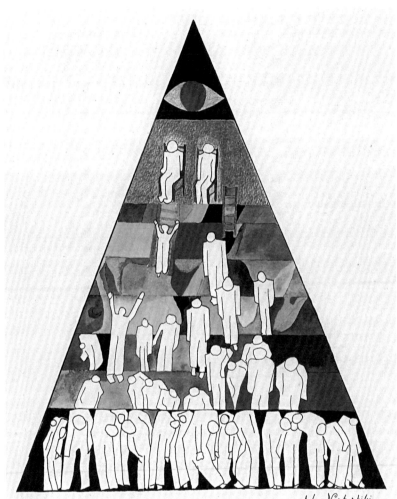

AL-Nashashibi
19 88

In School

In school I was told that history
Lives in the past
In my mind I believed that
History lives in the future
So I decided to write my own

In school I learned that science is logic
In my mind I thought that even
Science cannot explain the secret of
The creation of life

In school they said
Faith should be blindly followed
In my mind I had eyes to question
And seek answers

Now l am out of school
And fully confused

The History Nap

It's the year two thousand fourteen
Life is hard and the world is still in the hands of evil.
I am tired and confused, so I took a deep, long sleep.
When I woke up it was already the year two thousand fifty.
The sky was-healthy blue and the birds were singing with
no disruption.
global warming was fixed and politicians had solved the
world's problems.
Violence, wars and poverty were canceled from the
dictionary as obsolete.
All gained their dignity and freedom.
So human rights organizations celebrated their final
achievements and stored their reports away.
The world became one great nation and the people were
one family, all religions united in the love of one God, and God
blessed all.
My breath of joy was denied when my dream came to an end.
To continue my hopeful wish, I went back to sleep.

The Olive Tree

Could I be born as
A green branch
Of an olive tree
Planted in
Jerusalem

Would
My tears be its
Virgin oil

Or maybe
I am just
Its roots
Living
Thousands of
Years beneath her soil

To My Queen

Underneath your feet I lay my brow to pay respect
Underneath your feet I put my lips to kiss the ground
You are standing on
Beneath your soil I bury myself and feel the joy
Of becoming part of your legacy
In your veins and bones I will always provide my blood
To give you eternal life
And my pride to make you the Queen of Earth
My beloved mother Jerusalem.

In Jerusalem

In Jerusalem,
in a building that existed before the time we know
in a room the size of my bed
with a window the size of my palm, I was born
in a room with a ceiling centered with a dome
that has the shape of my grandfather's hat

In Jerusalem I received my emotions
and developed my personality
and there, still a child, I had a dream
a dream to live forever

So on a clear summer day
I secretly went down our dried well
and in its deepest corner I buried my message to the future

I, the son of humanity, invite all to share
love and peace
with our mother
Jerusalem

Thank You, San Diego

A bouquet of thanks goes to the people of San Diego
who embraced me as one of their loved ones
A sky of appreciation
Offered from my heart to those who acknowledged
And recognized the artist in me,
when I first brushed paint to paper
With great sincerity, gratitude and devotion
I convey my love to the charming and
Finest city San Diego
She sheltered me by delivering feelings of security and joy
Her spirituality enhanced my vision
And enriched my imagination
She is a gorgeous city that has four seasons in a single day
San Diego is the other name for Heaven

In Novi Sad

In Novi Sad
when I lived there
The snow
was the ruler and
The only enforcer

The room was so cold
and all night long
My body was
Shivering

In the morning
when I looked at the fog
in the Serbian sky
I discovered
the whole city
was
Shivering

A Dialog With Gandhi

Without a doubt you are
One of the heroes
In my chosen family
In my youth
I saw you as the king of peace
You still are
But now I don't see that your efforts
Gave a healthy birth to your
Baby of benevolence

A Free Spirit I Was Born

In youth
Because of my ignorance
I thought I was a bird
With wings to fly through
instead they taught me to crawl

In youth
Because of my ignorance
I thought I was a dove
To sing the sound of peace
Instead they told me I was a boy
And allowed only to cry
The bleeding heart of Gaza

The Orphan

In Jerusalem I was born
From love as my father and
From happiness as my mother
I had uncles created by joy
And aunts came from the light of
Tenderness

My childhood was tightly secured
So the stars were my muses
And the moon was my best friend
The sun gave my spirit the warmth I needed
To become the luckiest child

And now
Living my last days
Away from the womb of Jerusalem
Makes me aware
I am just an
Orphan
Wandering
The world

My Secret

My secret is simple
Just like my spirit
it can be discovered
through my work

When the muse visits
my imagination
I think of you
and feel as you feel
worried about our world

So you and I became
one family of peaceful power
armed with love
to spread the seeds of
secured joy and happiness
as a shield to protect humanity
from the Masters of
Destruction

The Muses Dancing Dabkeh

The Muses Harvesting The Grapes Of Hebron

The Muses Of Jerusalem

The Muses In The Flower Market

The Mother And The Child

The Embrace

The House Of Peace

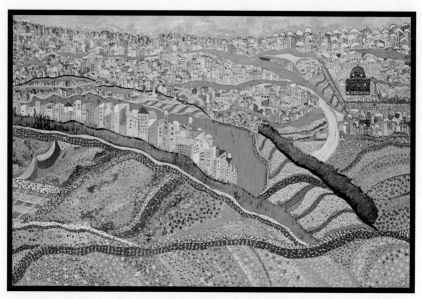

I Love Jerusalem

Silwan

Jerusalem My Love

Welcome To Jerusalem

The City Of Dreams

Al Taybeh One

Al Taybeh Two

The Alley Of Love

The Eye Of Enlightenment

Vincent Van Gogh

The Muses In The Presence Of The Prince

Waiting

The Muse Of Delegance

The Mother Of The Muses

The Muses In Via Dolorosa

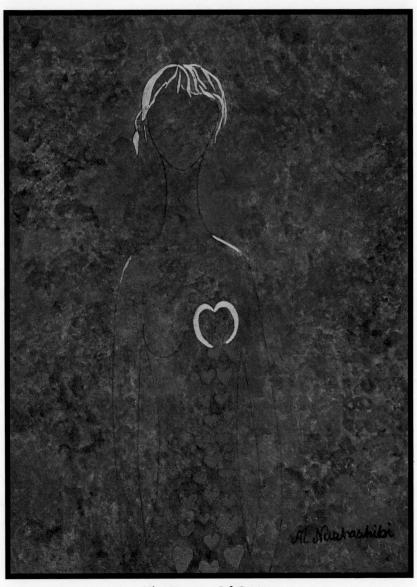

The Beauty Of Giving